Report No. SPO-2010-008   September 30, 2010

Inspector General
United States
Department *of* Defense

I0426187

Quality Assurance Review

of the

Defense Education Activity Hotline Program

INSPECTOR GENERAL
DEPARTMENT OF DEFENSE
400 ARMY NAVY DRIVE
ARLINGTON, VIRGINIA 22202-4704

SEP 3 0 2010

MEMORANDUM FOR DIRECTOR, DEFENSE EDUCATION ACTIVITY

SUBJECT: Quality Assurance Review of the Defense Education Activity Hotline Program
(Report No. SPO-2010-0008)

We are providing this report for your information and use. We performed the review consistent with the DoD Instruction 7050.01 "Defense Hotline Program," December 17, 2007, that requires the DoD Inspector General (DoD IG) to conduct periodic Quality Assurance Reviews (QAR) of DoD Component Hotline Programs. We considered management comments on a draft of the report in preparing the final report.

Comments on the draft of this report conformed to the requirements of DoD Directive 7650.3 and left no unresolved issues. Therefore, we do not require any additional comments.

We appreciate the courtesies extended to the staff. Please direct questions to me at (703) 604-9262 or Mr. Michael A. DiRenzo at (703) 604-9643 or Mr. William D. Means at (703) 604-9105.

Kenneth P. Moorefield
Deputy Inspector General
Special Plans and Operations

cc: Under Secretary of Defense for Personnel and Readiness

Results in Brief: Quality Assurance Review of the Defense Education Activity Hotline Program

What We Did

DoD Instruction 7050.01 "Defense Hotline Program," December 17, 2007, requires the DoD Inspector General (DoD IG) to conduct Quality Assurance Reviews (QAR) of DoD Component Hotline Programs. Specifically, the Inspector General of the Department of Defense, as the principal advisor to the Secretary of Defense on all matters relating to the detection and prevention of fraud, waste, abuse, and mismanagement, shall:

> Conduct periodic QARs of DoD Component implementation of the Defense Hotline and of Component hotlines, providing oversight and follow-up to ensure that reported allegations are appropriately evaluated and acted on and that the findings and conclusions of any inquiry are fully documented by the investigating organization.

We selected the Defense Education Activity (DODEA) for a QAR to verify that complaints were processed properly and that files contained adequate documentation to support Defense Hotline Completion Report findings and conclusions.

We reviewed 52 case files which included 28 cases referred by the DoD IG Hotline, and 24 cases internally generated by DODEA that were completed during the previous 12 to 18 months, from March 2008 to August 2009. We were able to complete reviews of 22 case files with information available in files at the DODEA Office of Compliance and Assistance. We requested additional information and documentation from DODEA for 30 cases from world-wide field offices where the hotline inquiries were conducted. DODEA was able to provide 18 of the 30 field files requested.

What We Found

We found that:

- The DODEA hotline staff did not comply with the DoDI 7050.01 requirement to submit written requests for extension, explaining the reason for the delay and the anticipated completion date when Hotline Completion Reports were not submitted within 90 days of referral for nine cases.

- Twelve case files did not contain complete documentation as required by DoDI 7050.01.

i

- Hotline Completion Reports (HCRs) were not prepared and submitted in six cases when required, and in six other cases, HCRs that were submitted either were incomplete or did not comply with DoDI 7050.01reporting requirements.

What We Recommend

The Director, DODEA, should strengthen DODEA internal hotline quality control procedures to ensure that:

- The DODEA Office of Compliance and Assistance establishes a system to monitor hotline cases to ensure that, for non-criminal investigations, HCRs are submitted within 90 days of referral, and if not completed within that timeframe that a written request for extension be submitted stating the reason for the delay and the anticipated completion date.

- The DODEA Office of Compliance and Assistance establishes a system to ensure that case files for completed DoD hotline cases are fully documented, support findings and conclusions, and are retained in accordance with DoDI 7050.01 and Washington Headquarters Services Administrative Instruction 15, Volume II.

- The DODEA Office of Compliance and Assistance conducts quality assurance reviews of completed hotline cases to ensure that in every case where an HCR is required, that an HCR satisfying the requirements of DoDI 7050.01 is prepared and provided to the Defense Hotline for referred cases, and that a HCR is prepared and provided to the DODEA office of Assistance and Compliance for internally generated cases.

Management Comments

The Acting Director, Defense Education Activity, concurred with our recommendations and provided responsive comments. See the recommendation table below.

Recommendations Table

Management	Recommendations Requiring comment	No Additional Comments Required
Director DODEA		A
Director DODEA		B.1, B.2

Table of Contents

Acronyms and Abbreviations

DODEA	Department of Defense Education Activity
DoDI	Department of Defense Instruction
HCR	Hotline Completion Report
OIG	Office of the Inspector General
QAR	Quality Assurance Review
USD (P&R)	Undersecretary of Defense for Personnel and Readiness

Objective

We announced this review on August 10, 2009 (Appendix A). In accordance with our responsibilities under DoDI 7050.01, we evaluated the DODEA Hotline Program to determine whether complaints were processed properly, timely, and that files contained adequate documentation to support Defense Hotline Completion Report findings and conclusions.

Background

The Defense Hotline

The Defense Hotline is an important avenue for reporting fraud, waste, abuse, and mismanagement. To date, the Defense Hotline has received more than 228,000 calls and letters.[1] As a result of Defense Hotline investigations, the Government has saved or recovered $425 million.[2] More importantly, many of the cases resulted in safer products and equipment for our Military personnel and Defense Department employees.

The Defense Hotline is a system wherein complaints are received, evaluated, investigated, and corrective measures are instituted when appropriate. The DoD IG Hotline staff refers complaints to the appropriate DoD Component. The Hotline staff reviews all completed investigations to ensure all aspects of the complaint were addressed, inquiries were conducted properly, and appropriate corrective actions were taken based on stated findings and conclusions. The Hotline staff also works closely with DoD Components to ensure that complaints are efficiently and effectively investigated and reported. Hotline operations and procedures are set forth in the DoD Instruction 7050.01,"Defense Hotline Program," December 17, 2007.

DoDI 7050.01states that the DoD IG shall:

> Conduct periodic QARs of DoD Component hotline programs in accordance with paragraph 5.1.3 to verify that complaints are processed properly and that files contain adequate documentation to support Defense Hotline Completion Report findings and conclusions. The QAR is an analysis of the quality of the inquiry based on the documentation contained in the completed hotline case file and an evaluation of the timeliness, independence, objectivity, and overall adequacy of the hotline inquiry.

> The QAR examines hotline inquiries completed during the previous 12 to 18 months, and includes cases referred to the DoD Component by the Defense Hotline and those received directly by the DoD Component hotline. The analysis focuses on compliance with policy and procedures, and on identification of systemic strengths or weaknesses in the manner in which the DoD Component conducts its inquiries.

---

[1] http://www.dodig.mil/HOTLINE/hotline1.htm accessed May 3, 2010.
[2] Ibid.

Referral for Action

Defense Hotline allegations referred to the DoD Component for action are allegations that shall be resolved by the DoD Component, may be an indication of a systemic problem within the Component, or have been determined through the Defense Hotline review process as requiring DoD Component attention.[3] In response to an allegation referred for action, the DoD Component shall conduct an inquiry and provide a Defense Hotline Completion Report to the Defense Hotline.

Referral for Information

Complaints or disagreements that do not require intervention by the DoD Component, but should be brought to the Component's attention are referred for information. These referrals do not require a Defense Hotline Completion Report unless the DoD Component decides to conduct an inquiry that results in corrective action.

The Defense Education Activity Hotline Program

The Office of Compliance and Assistance serves as DODEA's control point for all DoD IG hotline referrals and administrative investigations. The DODEA Office of Compliance and Assistance has the responsibility for ensuring that all hotline complaints receive appropriate attention, that all allegations are addressed, and that responses are provided to the DoD IG as required. The Office of Compliance and Assistance also receives referrals directly from DODEA internal sources, and maintains a tracking system for all hotline cases.

When the Office of Compliance and Assistance receives a complaint referral, they determine the nature of the complaint and forward the complaint to the appropriate management official for review. The Office of Compliance and Assistance staff assists program officials in determining the optimum manner to obtain information or evidence and report inquiry results.

---

[3] DoD Instruction 7050.01, "Defense Hotline Program," December 17, 2007.

Scope and Methodology

We conducted this review in accordance with the standards established by the President's Council on Integrity and Efficiency (now the Council of the Inspectors General on Integrity and Efficiency) published in the *Quality Standards for Inspections*, January 2005.

We developed a checklist (Appendix B) that we used to do the case analysis of hotline inquiries as part of our evaluation of the DODEA Hotline Program. Those inquiries included cases referred by the DoD IG Hotline Office to DODEA and self generated cases initiated within DODEA. We developed the checklist based on the documentation requirements for a Defense Hotline Completion Report, and QAR case evaluation criteria set forth in DoDI 7050.01, Enclosures 2 and 3, respectively. It provided a reasonable methodology to capture our observations and conclusions in concert with the review objectives. The elements in DoDI 7050.01 used to develop the checklist included such items as timeliness of inquiry, independence of investigator, case file documentation, and adequacy of inquiry. The checklist also includes the elements required to be included in Defense Hotline Completion Reports. Specifically, our analysis focused on compliance with policy and procedures and identification of systemic strengths or weaknesses in the manner in which the DODEA conducts inquiries.

We reviewed 52 case files which included 28 cases referred by the DoD IG Hotline, and 24 cases internally generated by DODEA that were completed during the previous 12 to 18 months, from March 2008 to August 2009. This represented all of the hotline cases completed by DODEA during that period. We were able to complete our review of 22 cases using files at the DODEA Office of Compliance and Assistance. We requested that the DODEA Office of Compliance and Assistance obtain supporting case files from the DODEA field offices for 30 case files for which there was incomplete documentation in the summary files located at the DODEA Office of Compliance and Assistance or the DoD IG Hotline Office. The DODEA Office of Compliance and Assistance was able to obtain 18 case files from field offices but reported that 12 case files were no longer available from the field offices for a variety of reasons.

The DoD IG Hotline cases referred for action or information that we reviewed are listed on tables 1 and 2, respectively.

Table 1. Cases Referred for Action by the DoD IG Hotline

Item	Case Number	Result of DODEA Investigation
1	88223	Not Substantiated
2	105508	Partially Substantiated
3	105968	Not Substantiated
4	106039	Not Substantiated
5	106403	Partially Substantiated
6	106477	Not Substantiated
7	106999	Not Substantiated
8	107793	Not Substantiated
9	108056	Not Substantiated
10	109325	Substantiated
11	110013	Partially Substantiated

Table 2. Cases Referred for Information by the DoD IG Hotline

Item	Case Number	Result of DODEA Investigation
1	104107	Substantiated
2	105278	No Action Required
3	106268	Substantiated
4	106432	No Action Required
5	106785	Substantiated
6	106921	No Action Required
7	107305	Partially Substantiated
8	108000	No Action Required
9	108405	Partially Substantiated
10	108617	No Action Required
11	108902	Not Substantiated
12	108939	No Action Required
13	109157	Partially Substantiated
14	109215	Not Substantiated
15	110061	No Action Required
16	111249	Not Substantiated
17	107125	No Action Required

DODEA internally generated cases that we reviewed are listed on Table 3.

Table 3. DoDEA Internally Generated Cases

Item	Case Number	Result of DODEA Investigation
1	77-08	Substantiated
2	117-08	Not Substantiated
3	146-08	Not Substantiated
4	195-08	Not Substantiated
5	218-08	Not Substantiated
6	231-08	Not Substantiated
7	273-08	Not Substantiated
8	280-08	Partially Substantiated
9	362-08	Not Substantiated
10	383-08	Not Substantiated
11	384-08	Partially Substantiated
12	437-08	Not Substantiated
13	444-08	Not Substantiated
14	20-09	Not Substantiated
15	52-09	Partially Substantiated
16	58-09	Not Substantiated
17	63-09	Not Substantiated
18	105-09	Not Substantiated
19	104-09	Not Substantiated
20	143-09	Partially Substantiated
21	160-09	Not Substantiated
22	180-09	Partially Substantiated
23	240-09	Not Substantiated
24	329-09	Not Substantiated

Results – Cases Not in Compliance with DoDI 7050.01.

Twenty one of 52 cases reviewed did not meet all of the DoDI 7050.01 requirements, including those for timeliness, reporting, and documentation. Those cases are listed and discussed in findings sections A and B.

A. Timeliness of Completed Inquiries

DoD Instruction 7050.01, paragraph 6.2.5 requires that DoD Component Hotline Coordinators:

> Prepare a Defense Hotline Completion Report using the format in Enclosure 2, and submit it to the Defense Hotline through the DoD Coordinator within 90 days (180 days for criminal investigations and audits) from the date the complaint was transmitted by the Defense Hotline. When necessary, requests for extensions of these timeframes shall be in writing to the Defense Hotline stating the reason for the delay and the anticipated completion date.

The DODEA Office of Compliance and Assistance did not have an adequate process to monitor hotline cases to ensure that, for non-criminal hotline investigations, HCRs are submitted within 90 days of receipt, or that when an investigation exceeds 90 days ensure that a written request for extension is submitted stating the reason for the delay and the anticipated completion date.

We found that for 6 of 11 cases that were referred for action by the Defense Hotline, written requests for extension were not submitted when the investigations were not completed within 90 days. In 3 internally generated cases, the DODEA Office of Compliance and Assistance hotline coordinator did not ensure completion or document the granting of an extension for internally generated cases. Those 9 cases that took over 90 days to complete are listed on Tables 4 and 5 below for DoD IG Defense Hotline referred and DODEA internally generated cases, respectively.

Table 4. DoD IG Referred Cases Over 90 Days
Without Request for Extension

Item	Case Number	Number of Days to Complete
1	88223	No closing date reported*
2	105508	148
3	106039	410
4	106477	230
5	107793	98
6	109325	139

* Closed by the Defense Hotline May 18, 2008

Table 5. DoDEA Internally Generated Cases Over 90 Days
Without Request for Extension

Item	Case Number	Number of Days to Complete
1	20-09	199
2	52-09	133
3	63-09	99

Recommendations, Management Comments, and Our Response

A. Timeliness of Completed Inquiries

We recommend that the Director, DODEA, strengthen DODEA internal hotline quality control procedures to ensure that the DODEA Office of Compliance and Assistance establishes a system to monitor hotline cases to ensure that, for non-criminal hotline investigations, HCRs are submitted within 90 days receipt, and if not completed within that timeframe prescribed by DoDI 7050.01, that for:

a. cases referred by the DoD IG, submit a written request for extension to the DoD Hotline stating the reason for the delay and the anticipated completion date;

b. cases generated internally, ensure completion of documentation stating reason for delay and request for extension from DODEA Office of Compliance and Assistance.

Defense Education Activity Comments

The Acting Director, Defense Education Activity, concurred with comment, and stated that the DoDEA Office of Compliance and Assistance will ensure that hotline inquiries are completed within 90 days of receipt. If not completed within that timeframe, written requests for an extension will be submitted to the DoD IG stating the reason for the delay and the anticipated completion date.

Our Response

The Acting Director, Defense Education Activity comments are responsive. No additional comments are required.

B. Case File Documentation

Finding B.1 - Working Paper Support

DoD Instruction 7050.01 provides guidance to investigators on the types of data and documents which should be included in case files. DoD Instruction 7050.01, paragraph 6.2.6, requires that each Defense Hotline case file contain documentation that supports the hotline inquiry findings and conclusions. This includes the Defense Hotline referral, the Defense Hotline Completion Report, when required, a description of the actions taken by the examining official to determine the findings, the complete identity of all witnesses, the dates of and information relayed during interviews, specific details, and locations of all documents reviewed during the examination, and a description of any other actions the DoD Component took as a result of the inquiry.

Washington Headquarters Services (WHS) Administrative Instruction (AI) 15, Volume II, Subject: Office of the Secretary of Defense (OSD) Records Management Program – Records Disposition Schedules, April 18, 2008 states that Grievance, Disciplinary, and Adverse Action Files are to be retained for at least 4 years after final decision and may be destroyed thereafter but no later than 7 years after the case is closed. [4]

As previously noted, for 30 of the 52 allegations reviewed there was incomplete documentary evidence in the case files located at the DODEA Office of Compliance and Assistance to fully support investigator findings and conclusions in conformance with DoDI 7050.01. We requested the complete case files containing the working papers for these 30 cases from the field offices where the inquiries were conducted be provided by DODEA. DODEA Office of Compliance and Assistance was able to provide additional documentation for 18 case files, but was unable to provide additional information for 12 case files because examining officials who conducted the inquiries had either transferred or retired, but did not leave complete working paper files. Those 12 cases are listed in Table 6.

Table 6. Incomplete Case Files

Item	Case Number
1	88223
2	105278
3	106477
4	106785
5	106999
6	108056
7	108405
8	108939
9	109157
10	77-08
11	20-09
12	329-09

---

[4] Washington Headquarters Service Administrative Instruction 15, Volume II, Subject: Office of the Secretary of Defense (OSD) Records Management Program – Records Disposition Schedules, April 18, 2008, section 202-49 page 44.

RECOMMENDATION B.1

We recommend that the Director, DODEA, require the Office of Compliance and Assistance to establish a system to ensure that case files for completed DoD hotline cases are fully documented, support findings and conclusions, and are retained in accordance with DoDI 7050.01 and WHS AI 15, Volume II.

Defense Education Activity Comments

The Acting Director, Defense Education Activity, concurred with comment, and stated that during the course of the review it was determined that some investigative working papers (case file documentation), which are normally retained by the assigned investigator were not available due to personnel transfers and retirements. The Acting Director reaffirmed that in the future, DoDEA will ensure that working papers will be electronically scanned and retained at both the Area Office and Headquarters level.

Our Response

The Acting Director, Defense Education Activity's comments are responsive. No additional comments are required.

FINDING B.2 Hotline Completion Reports

The DODEA Office of Compliance and Assistance does not have an adequate process to ensure that Hotline Completion Reports (HCR) are prepared for every case by the investigating official or the DODEA Office of Compliance and Assistance Hotline staff. Further, the DODEA Office of Compliance and Assistance does not have an adequate process for ensuring that Hotline Completion Reports that have been prepared are complete and comply with DoDI 7050.01 when forwarded to the DoD IG Defense Hotline.

We determined that 41 of the 52 allegations reviewed required preparation of an HCR in accordance with DoDI 7050.01, paragraphs 3.2 and 3.3, and Enclosure 2. They included 15 cases referred for action, 2 cases referred for information where the allegations were partially substantiated, and all 24 DODEA internally generated cases. We considered internally generated cases for processing as referred for action.

We found that twelve cases did not comply with DoDI 70501.01 requirements for HCRs. For six cases there was no HCR prepared. In 6 of 35 cases where HCRs were prepared, they did not comply with the requirements of DoDI 7050.01. Those cases are listed on Tables 7 and 8.

Table 7. DoD IG Referred Cases - No/Incomplete HCR

Item	Case Number	Reason for Noncompliance
1	106999	No HCR Prepared
2	108405	Incomplete HCR
3	106432	Incomplete HCR
4	106268	Incomplete HCR
5	106403	Incomplete HCR
6	109157	Incomplete HCR

Table 8. DODEA Internally Generated Cases – No/Incomplete HCR

Item	Case Number	Reason for Noncompliance
1	77-08	No HCR Prepared
2	20-09	No HCR Prepared
3	240-09	No HCR Prepared
4	329-09	No HCR Prepared
5	63-09	No HCR Prepared
6	52-09	Incomplete HCR

RECOMMENDATION B.2

We recommend that the Director, DODEA, strengthen DODEA internal hotline quality control procedures to ensure that in every case where an HCR is required, that a HCR satisfying the requirements of DoDI 7050.01 is prepared and provided to the:

a. Defense Hotline for referred cases; and

b. DODEA office of Assistance and Compliance for internally generated cases.

Defense Education Activity Comments

The Acting Director, Defense Education Activity, concurred with comment, and stated that DoDEA will establish a schedule for conducting periodic Quality Assurance Reviews (QAR) with each of their Area Offices and that QARs can be conducted in conjunction with periodic investigations training that is provided to each of the DoDEA Areas. The Acting Director stated further that DoDEA Office of Compliance will also ensure that Hotline Completion Reports are completed on hotline cases as required by DoDI 7050.01

Our Response

The Acting, Director Defense Education Activity, comments are responsive. No additional comments are required.

Appendix A – DoDEA Announcement Letter

INSPECTOR GENERAL
DEPARTMENT OF DEFENSE
400 ARMY NAVY DRIVE
ARLINGTON, VIRGINIA 22202-4704

AUG 1 0 2009

MEMORANDUM FOR DIRECTOR, DEFENSE EDUCATION ACTIVITY

SUBJECT: Quality Assurance Review of the Defense Education Activity Hotline
Program (D2009-DIP0E1-0273.000)

We will begin the subject review in August 2009. DoD Instruction 7050.01,
"Defense Hotline Program," December 17, 2007, requires that the DoD Inspector General
conduct Quality Assurance Reviews (QAR) of DoD Component Hotline Programs, "to
verify that complaints are processed properly and that files contain adequate
documentation to support Defense Hotline Completion Report findings and conclusions."

We have selected the Defense Education Activity (DoDEA) for a Hotline QAR. In
preparation for the review, please provide the following information by August 31, 2009:

- DoDEA Hotline Program policies and all other implementing guidance;
- Position descriptions of DoDEA personnel assigned to Hotline Program activities;
- A listing of all Hotline complaints, excluding those referred by the DoD Hotline,
  investigated and closed by your office since February 1, 2008.

We will review the case files of all Hotline inquiries completed by your Activity
from February 1, 2008, to date. If your records disposition procedures require the
destruction of hotline case files two years after case closure, please hold those procedures
in abeyance until after completion of our QAR. It is important that for this review, your
case files are in the same condition with all content that existed in the files at time of
closure by your Activity.

Please provide contact information for your DoD Hotline Coordinator and the above
requested information to our points of contact, Mr. Michael A DiRenzo, 703-604-9643,
(michael.direnzo@dodig.mil) or Mr. William D Means, 703-604-9105,
(william.means@dodig.mil).

Charles W. Beardall
Deputy Inspector General
for Policy and Oversight

Appendix B – Checklist for Reviewing Closed Hotline Files

			Inspector Comments
	DoD Hotline Case Number		
	Quality Assurance Review Completion Date & Time		
A	**Hotline Completion Report (HCR)/Report of Investigation (ROI)—DoDI 7050.01—E2.2**		
A.1	What is the Inquiry Officials name? (Last, First, Middle Initial)		
A.2	What is their Rank (and component) or Grade?		
A.3	What is their duty position name?		
A.4	What is their telephone number?		
A.5	What is their organization?		
A.6	What is the case number (Hotline Control Number)?		
A.7	What is the subject of the inquiry?		
A.8	What is the Referral Code? (Action or Information)		
A.1	**Scope of Inquiry, Findings, Conclusions, and Recommendations)—DoDI 7050.01—E2.2.6**		
A.1.1	**E2.2.6.1. Scope of Inquiry**		
A.1.2	Did the HCR contain a statement of the allegations and identify the organization and location, the person or persons against whom the allegation was made?		
A.1.3	Did the HCL identify scope, nature and manner of inquiry including documents reviewed, witnesses interviewed for the scope, nature, and manner of the inquiry conducted?		
A.1.4	Were the inquiries or interviews conducted by telephone or in person?		
A.1.5	**E2.2.6.2. Findings**		
A.1.6	Did the findings relate to each allegation?		
A.1.7	Was the identity of interviewees documented in the official file of the component conducting the inquiry?		
A.1.8	Did the finding provides a list of documents and/or evidence collected to support the findings?		
A.1.9	**E2.2.6.3. Conclusions and Recommendations**		
A.1.10	Did the the official conducting the inquiry state the analysis of the findings and the conclusions for each allegation?		
A.1.11	Does the HCR/ROI state whether each allegation against each subject was substantiated, not substantiated or unfounded?		
A.1.12	Does the HCR/ROI include comments regarding the adequacy of existing policy or regulations?		
A.1.1	Does the HCR/ROI note weaknesses in internal control systems?		
A.1.1	Are there any recommended corrective actions noted?		
A.1.15	**E2.2.7. Criminal or Regulatory Violations Substantiated**		
A.1.16	For inquiries involving economy and efficiency, does the HCR contain a statement of management actions taken?		
A.1.17	For inquiries involving criminal or other unlawful acts, does the HCR include the results of criminal prosecutions and provide details of all charges and sentences imposed; the results of administrative actions, reprimands, the value of property or money recovered, or other such actions taken to prevent		
A.1.1	Does the HCR contain the proper security markings?		
A.1.1	Does the HCR contain the location of field working papers and files?		
B	**TIMELINESS OF INQUIRY—DoDI 7050.01—E3.1. & (6.2.5)**		Inspector Comments
B.1	HCR/ROI Received Date		
B.2	Referred/Closed Date Use Referred date for cases referred by DoD IG.		
B.3	Total days (using julean calendar) to process the case?		
B.4	Was the HCR/ROI submitted to the DoD Hotline within 90 days (180 days for criminal investigations and audits) from the date the complaint was transmitted by the DoD OIG Hotline?		
B.5	Did the DoD Component Hotline Coordinator request an extension(s) in writing?		
B.6	Did the HCR/ROI state the reason for the extension?		
B.7	Did the HCR/ROI provide anticipated completion date?		
B.8	Was the extension approved?		
B.9	Is length of processing time justified by complexity of complaint?		
B.10	Based upon B.3 thru B.9 is the HCR/ROI considered timely?		

		Inspector Comments
C	**INDEPENDENCE OF INVESTIGATOR—DoDI 7050.01—(E.3.2)**	
C.1	Was the Investigation Officer (IO) independent of *personal* impairments?	
C.2	Was the IO independent of *external* impairments?	
C.3	Was the IO independent of *organizational* impairments?	
C.4	Is the IO a *subordinate* of the individual whom the allegations are against?	
C.5	Is the HCR/ROI case reviewer independent?	
C.6	Is the HCR/ROI case review organization independent?	
C.7	Were legal opinions or technical expertise solicted when appropriate?	
C.8	Was the attorney performing the legal review a different individual then one assigned to advise the IO (and not a subordinate of that individual)?	
D	**CASE FILE DOCUMENTATION—DoDI 7050.01-E3.3. (6.2.6)**	Inspector Comments
D.1	Did the HCR/ROI identify the complainant?	
D.2	Did the HCR/ROI contain a statement of the allegation(s)?	
D.3	Did the HCR/ROI identify organization & location at time of allegation?	
D.4	Did the HCR/ROI identify person(s) against whom allegation(s) was/were	
D.5	Did the HCR/ROI describe scope, nature & manner of inquiry conducted?	
D.6	Did the HCR/ROI include all of the documents used in the review?	
D.7	Did the HCR/ROI contain location of working papers and files?	
D.8	Was there evidence of an investigation plan in (field) file?	
D.9	Were witnesses interviewed?	
D.10	How were interviews conducted (telephone or in person)?	
D.11	Were there adequate notes from statements/testimony supporting conclusion?	
D.12	Did the HCR/ROI discuss mitigating circumstances?	
D.13	Did documentation support findings/conclusion?	
D.14	Did it appear that the preponderance of evidence standard was applied?	
D.15	Can the report stand alone without referring to supporting documents?	
D.16	Did the HCR/ROI contain the DoD Hotline case number?	
D.17	Did the HCR/ROI contain the proper security markings?	
D.18	Was the completed HCR/ROI forwarded to the Directing Authority with all appropriate command/management endorsements?	
E	**ADEQUACY OF INQUIRY—DoDI 7050.01-E3.4.**	Inspector Comments
E.1	Were all the allegations in the basic complaint addressed	
E.2	Were all key individuals (witnesses and subjects) interviewed?	
E.3	Were all relevant questions asked?	
E.4	Did the Investigating Officer collect and review all pertinent documentation in support of his conclusions?	
E.5	Were legal opinions or technical expertise solicited when appropriate?	
E.6	Did the examining official demonstrate a "common sense" approach while conducting this inquiry?	
E.7	Is the case considered adequate?	
F	**Recommended Action (I&E Inspector(s) Conclusion)**	Inspector Comments
F.1	Does the case review satisfy DoD Instruction 7050.01?	
F.2	Should the case be reopened and reassigned?	
F.3	Do you have another recommendation? **NOTE: If yes, attach to checklist!**	
	Name of DoD IG Evaluator =====>	
	Signature of Evaluator =====>	

14

Appendix C – Management Comments

DEPARTMENT OF DEFENSE
EDUCATION ACTIVITY
4040 NORTH FAIRFAX DRIVE
ARLINGTON, VA 22203-1635

SEP - 9 2010

MEMORANDUM FOR DEPUTY INSPECTOR GENERAL FOR SPECIAL PLANS
AND OPERATIONS

SUBJECT: Quality Assurance Review (QAR) of the Department of Defense Education
Activity (DoDEA) Hotline Program

We appreciate the opportunity to comment on the subject report. Our responses to the
recommendations contained in the report are noted below:

Recommendation: *The DoDEA Office of Compliance and Assistance establishes a
system to monitor hotline cases to ensure that, for non-criminal investigations, hotline inquiries
are completed within 90 days of receipt, and if not completed within that timeframe that a
written request for extension be submitted stating the reason for the delay and the anticipated
completion date.*

RESPONSE: Concur with comment. The DoDEA Office of Compliance and
Assistance will ensure that hotline inquiries are completed within 90 days of receipt, and if not
completed within that timeframe, written requests for an extension will be submitted stating the
reason for the delay and the anticipated completion date. It should be noted that DoDEA
investigations, most of which are at the school level, are constrained by the school calendar in
that much investigative activity can not take place during school breaks and the summer months.
The DoD Hotline staff is well aware of this limitation. It is also important to note that DoD
Hotline referrals are often not received in a timely manner, therefore causing a delay in starting
the investigation. Our analysis of DoD Hotlines from July 2008 to present shows that it takes
approximately 170 days on average from the time a hotline complaint is received by the DoD
Hotline until it is referred to DoDEA. This timeframe ranged from six days to over eleven
months to reach DoDEA. DoD Hotline assistance in expediting the front end of the hotline
referral process will help DoDEA in providing timely and responsive inquiries.

Recommendation: *The DoDEA Office of Compliance and Assistance establishes a
system to ensure that case files for completed DoD hotline cases are fully documented, support
findings and conclusions, and are retained in accordance with DoDI 7050.01 and Washington
Headquarters Services Instruction 15, Volume II.*

RESPONSE: Concur with comment. During the course of the review it was determined
that some investigative working papers (case file documentation) which are normally retained by
the assigned investigator were not available due to personnel transfers and retirements. In the
future, DoDEA will ensure that working papers will be electronically scanned and retained at
both the Area Office and Headquarters level.

The finding discussion concerning retention of files is not clear. Both the DoDI 7050.01 and WHS AI 15, Vol. II do not discuss a Hotline Program. The only possible applicable reference in WHS AI 15, Vol. II is para. 202-49 Grievance, Disciplinary, and Adverse Action Files. Hotline files do not meet the definition for Grievance, Disciplinary, or Adverse Action. It is recommended that, in order to comply with this recommendation, DoDEA use the DoD Inspector General Instruction 5015.2, Chapter 8, para. 840, Hotline Referral Files. Emulating the records management requirements of the DoD Hotline Program would comply with this recommendation.

Recommendation: The DoDEA Office of Compliance and Assistance conducts quality assurance reviews of completed hotline cases to ensure that in every case where an HCR is required, that an HCR satisfying the requirements of DoDI 7050.01 is prepared and provided to the Defense Hotline for referred cases, and that an HCR is prepared and provided to the DoDEA Office of Compliance and Assistance for internally generated cases.

RESPONSE: Concur with comment. DoDEA will establish a schedule for conducting periodic Quality Assurance Reviews (QAR) with each of our Area Offices. QARs can be conducted in conjunction with periodic investigations training that is provided to each of the DoDEA Areas. We will also ensure that Hotline Completion Reports (HCR) are completed on hotline cases as required by DoDI 7050.01. It should be noted that some "cases" are in actuality non-referral issues that are appropriately documented and closed based upon preliminary analysis. These issues are typically without basis, unfounded, or have been previously addressed and documented in an appropriate forum. We maintain that this is an appropriate practice and done in consultation with the DoD Hotline staff.

We will implement the above recommendations within 120 days. Finally, we believe that the overall quality of the DoDEA Hotline program is high and our feedback from the DoD Hotline staff has been positive and marked by an excellent working relationships.

My point of contact on this matter is Mr. Robert Blewis, Chief of Staff, who may be contacted by e-mail at: robert.blewis@hq.dodea.edu or by telephone at (703) 588-3303.

Marilee Fitzgerald
Acting Director

2

www.ingramcontent.com/pod-product-compliance
Lightning Source LLC
Chambersburg PA
CBHW081153290526
45795CB00008B/2906